Haiku In The Life Of You:

Family, Friends and Falling In Love

By D.W. Hirsch

Be social and follow my adventures:

Instagram: @dwhirsch

Facebook: DWHirsch, Author

X: @DWHirsch

Bluesky: @dwhirsch.bsky.social

Website: D.W.Hirsch Writes https://www.dwhirschwrites.com

Cover art designed by probook designs
Formatted by www.bookclaw.com

Thanks to Jacki, who inspired this and all future collections.

To my friends--Deb, Leah, Roomie, Tina and others-- for being a part of my life.

To my parents. You are remembered more than you know.

As always, to my husband who gives me a
"You go, girl!"
every day of my life, a great gift.

TABLE OF CONTENTS

INTRODUCTION

My college friend and I were inspired by a book we read to challenge each other to mail daily postcards and write a haiku on each. What started in the late 1990s continues today through both snail mail and email.

Traditional Haiku poems are a 3-line poetic style from Japan that explore nature and the seasons. Senryu is a similar style that focuses on everyday interactions and observations. We incorporated both into our poems using the common 5-7-5 syllable format and a 3-5-3 syllable format she created.

My style is an approach to a personal journal. The haiku I write celebrate relationships, humorous anecdotes, serious thoughts and playful moments of the world around me. These short sentiments are insights into my life at the time, moments that are still relevant today. The way I look at the world now surprises me. Life changes, but it doesn't change. Pause and look at the world around you.

This haiku collection was written between the years 2000 - 2013. During this time, I worked in full-time professional jobs. My parents grew older and departed this world. My friends moved away for their jobs and life. I met the man who would become my husband. These snapshot memoir moments relate to the world now as they did then. Join me in experiencing the connection we all share with the people in our lives.

Teddy bears

soak up your tears so

heart won't break.

FAMILY

FAMILY - MOTHER

Kitten held
in palm. Mother, I
understand.

Mom's message, saw first
Mourning Dove. Mother dove. No
birds here. Is it Spring?

Childhood Japanese
stickers remind me of Mom,
Hello Kitty days.

Mom's wreath pin with bell
ching-cling reminds me she is
getting angel wings

"I Am the Bread Of Life"

Communion song. Mom's
Funeral. People, don't stare
Let me cry myself.

As I cramp, my friend
grows a baby. I wonder
what it feels like. "Mom"

Admission, thirty
six dollars. Two hours, lunch,
Mom's deep hug: priceless

FAMILY - FATHER

My father's phone call
ends "I Love You." Rarely says.
Why now? Something wrong?

Crossing street, Dad holds
my hand. Gentleman? Manners?
Dad, I'll remember

Grey-haired man, Sudoku
book, coffeeshop. Could be Dad
reading newspaper.

Street with no sidewalk.
We walk. I'm house side, he's on
Dad side of the street.

Father. Playground. Boy.
"Higher! Push higher!" his feet
almost touch tree leaves.

old man, grocery
store: "Your smile is lovely." smile
more, Dad would say that

Dad. Me. Dance.
Wedding. Video.
All. Remains.

FAMILY - FAMILY MEMBERS

Black and white photos
crisp through today's color eyes
who are these faces?

On my lap,
Baby's hair, clean smell
Of future

Want alone, want
a nap, family vacation
Not to be wasted

"Stop splash!" "Why?"
he whimpers "My
feet are wet."

Precious baby drool
pools on my shoulder after
singing her to sleep.

Grandma chews Coffee
Nibs one at a time, that's how
I remember her

Green metal box. Post
cards. Foreign coins. Keys, to what?
Grandpa's legacy.

FAMILY - MEMORIES

Discovered photos
I didn't know I had. Smiles
Me now, pictures then

Ripped, stained cardboard box
under sweatshirt, 21st
Birthday, Love Mom Dad

Cabinet shelf, Herr's
No-Salt Potato Chips burnt
orange bag left behind.

Missing book. Missing
Marriage license. Missing Pen
Case. Missing my mind.

Crack in lamp
dog knocked over I
never fixed

Inherit coffee
cup. Dusty inside, no one
drank coffee from it.

Grandma's diamond ring.
Dad's wedding band. Mom's beadwork.
A pirate's treasure.

FRIENDS

FRIENDS - MUSIC & GAMES

Disco lights, flash, beat,
feet, shoulders, bump, thump, bounce, sing
lyrics we can't hear

Air hockey. She scores
first goal, wags her tongue at me.
I score last goal. Smirk.

On the Radio

High school song.
We did what we did
to music

Square Peg, April 2013

Go away, waiter.
No drinks. We're playing Jenga.
Need concentration.

June 30th

Windows down, heat on
singing "It's Raining Men" at
the tops of our lungs.

Almost win
then Yahtzee is rolled
on last turn

Coffeeshop Scrabble.
Egg. Puz. Eroded.
Quid. (triple letter Q) Joy.

FRIENDS - "TWO FRIENDS"

Two friends talk and talk
until 11 o'clock
chases home, walk, walk

Two friends sit in car.
Silence is all that's needed
yet I talk through it.

Two friends celebrate
with lunch, savor quiet bench
sharing both good gifts

Two friends hold photo
now of moment then. What does
the other one think?

Two friends nap
on couch and chair as
movie ends

Two friends walk around
block, wander again, again
being together

Two friends on barstools
slice hushed hotel lobby loud
Vodka Collins laugh

FRIENDS - DEATH AND BETRAYAL

Dear Monday,

"How are you?" "Better,
my dad died Friday." *Sorry*
feels inadequate.

Rosey

Her dog's sleeping now
after one long joyful romp.
I cry for my friend.

Hospital on hill
She dies there. Nurse comforts "We're
not meant to forget."

Unexpected web
search. Her. Affair, yes. Friendship,
no. Do I still care?

Her friend died last week.
I text her: "Coffee's on me."
"Herbal tea thank you"

"I miss puppy," he
says, "and parents. Don't know how
much time we have left."

Friend's note: Family
death, thankful what's left, could
be worse. Reminder.

FRIENDS - BEING TOGETHER

Best friends say all that
is needed with their eyes and
the touch of a hand.

I would ride crowded
smelly bus stuck in traffic
to have lunch with you

A long talk, parking
lot, lean against our cars
Friendship by streetlight

Share the love.
Be a friend to them.
Friend yourself.

Cross-stitching at night
We talk while baby fusses
Tina shares her thread.

We talk for
hours, not saying
much at all

"Be nice to me, I
Have all our college photos."
Trust is in her smile.

FALLING IN LOVE

FALLING IN LOVE
- THE BEGINNING

Silent winter path
our white sneakers crunch snow. Right
Left. Right. Together.

faraway worries
does he like me? will he call?
then you do. my yes.

Chill outdoor garden
Wind shivers my shoulders.
You Drape me in your coat

Street with no sidewalk
he walks on my left, outside
just like my father.

Hug beside fountain
Rushing water in one ear
Heartbeat in other

Sunday Night movie
What could be more simple and
more complicated?

Crowded. Smoky. Bar.
Loud. Band. You. Kiss. Me. Whisper.
My name. I hear you.

FALLING IN LOVE
- SAYING "I LOVE YOU"

Stop red light.
You lean kiss lips warm
I love you.

"I haven't told you
in last 5 minutes that I
love you." then you do.

"Did you know?" I ask.
"No," he replies. I wonder
I love you or not.

Cat pounces
crept up from nowhere
I love you

After lunch phone call
"to say I love you from the
bottom of my heart."

You walk in, smell like
spilled cologne bottle. For me?
I hope I love you.

"I love you."
"I love you, too." Then
life goes on.

FALLING IN LOVE - TOGETHER US

Two Syllable Word:
"Girlfriend." Ten letters with a
meaning much larger

you draw our
initials in sand
with long twig

Our spontaneous
parking lot laughter, others
here hear, hope jealous

Walk in a park by
dusk light we see each other
hold hands with our smile

Friday

9pm walk, out
open window stereo
blasts "Dead or Alive"

yell. cry. shout.
stare. apologize.
hug. kiss. kiss.

Walking to bus stop
middle-age couple hold hands
the entire way

FALLING IN LOVE - WEDDINGS

Four maroon bridesmaids
huddle in church nook. Sleeveless
bride gives frozen smile.

Mom: "Want my wedding
gown?" Let's tear apart the house
to find your white lace.

Bride trips down church stairs
Pity sad embarrassment
What is she thinking?

Las Vegas buffet.
Wide woman white lace gown asks
"Where are macaroons?"

Groom dashes
into drugstore, buys
one Chapstick

Our glasses
cling-cling, we kiss kiss
together

I sell my car to
myself for name change. Hope I
gave me a good deal.

WTC

Lonely. In three days
we reunite. Three thousand
not as fortunate.

ABOUT THE AUTHOR

D.W. Hirsch was born and raised in Pittsburgh, PA. At age 3, she completed her first book, an illustrated tale about Noah's Ark. The giraffes did not show bright on the paper with the yellow markers used, but disappointment never frustrated this writer.

This award-winning writer has published articles in newspapers and magazines, writing on a variety of subjects from travel to personality profiles to arts & crafts.

She is a Certified Zentangle Teacher. All Zentangle images included in this book are the original artwork created by the author.

OTHER BOOKS BY D.W. HIRSCH:

Star Trek, Mom and Las Vegas: A Grand Adventure

For more adventure, come along and roam her website: www.dwhirschwrites.com

Made in United States
North Haven, CT
09 June 2025